Contents

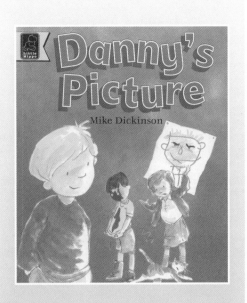

Changing moods

Learning objective
✳ To realize the purpose of illustrating a story and to understand that pictures, as well as print, carry meaning.

Theme links
✳ All about me

Group size: Whole group.

What you need
A copy of the book *Danny's Picture*; a blackboard or whiteboard; chalks or marker pens.

What to do
Begin by reading through the story with the children. Look carefully at Danny's first drawing of himself. Notice particularly the eyes/eyebrows and mouth. Reproduce the drawing on the blackboard/whiteboard, seeking the children's approval that you have done it correctly. Ask the children to describe the person in the picture. Is he happy or sad? Is he angry or in a good mood? How do they know? What features on the drawing tell them?

Now, consider the second drawing together. Again, look particularly at the eyes and mouth. Invite one child to alter your board drawing to match. What did they change? Ask them to describe this person. Has his character changed? In the third picture, the face has changed again and so has the mood of the person. Once more, ask for alterations to your picture and verbal responses about the person in Danny's picture.

The fourth drawing shows a very cross and grumpy person. What features tell us this? Do you think this person is nice or nasty? Is he being friendly or is he upsetting all his friends?

Invite the children to tell you what Danny might be saying in any of the drawings of him. For example, in the first picture, he looks happy and calm and might be saying 'Look everyone, I've done a good drawing of me'. In the last picture, he is sticking out his tongue rudely and looking very cross and grumpy, so he might be saying 'I hate you Austin and I'm glad I put paint in your boot. I don't care if I've upset you'.

Why did Danny's drawing change in this way? In the second half of the story, why did his drawing change back again?

Support
Ask the children to imitate the various drawings of Danny. How do they feel when they are making the different faces? Do they think Danny was feeling the same?

Extension
Give the children three very simple sentences, such as 'I fell over', 'I have sweets' and 'Sam hit me'. Ask them to draw pictures of themselves showing how they feel (sad, happy, angry) to illustrate the pieces of writing.

early years
Story box

What shall we write?

Learning objective
✳ To understand various purposes of writing and to identify different types of writing.

Theme links
✳ All about me

Group size: Whole group.

What you need
A copy of the photocopiable sheet on page 20 for each child; paper; pencils; erasers; pens; letters from friends; used postcards; greetings cards; lists; invitations; recipe books; used stamps.

What to do
When Danny gets home from school, his mother sticks his picture onto the fridge door. Beside it is some writing. What sort of writing do the children think it might be? Why do we write lists? Discuss shopping lists and 'to do' lists. If the children were going to go and buy the ingredients for making some little cakes, what might their list say? (Consult recipe books if necessary!) What other reasons for writing have the children come across?

Talk about Danny's picture which has his name written on it in order to identify it. Now look at and read some of the letters you have collected. Why do people write letters? Perhaps the children have written letters to say thank you for a present, to say sorry for a mistake or to give a friend some news. Allow plenty of time for discussion and encourage everyone to contribute their own ideas and experiences.

Now look at some of the greeting cards and invitations. People send cards to celebrate birthdays or other special events. Who have the children sent cards to? When? What did they write inside the card? Why do people write invitations? What might an invitation say? It must include details of when and where the party is and might include information about the type of party or why it is being given. Can the children suggest the wording for an invitation to a birthday party? Can they suggest the wording for a letter replying to that invitation? Why do people sometimes send postcards, rather than write letters? When we are on holiday, our friends like to see where we are as well as being told about our news, so we often send postcards with pictures of where we are.

Provide each child with an A5 piece of card and ask them to write their own postcard. Encourage them to draw their own picture on the card, to 'write' a message on the back and to 'send' it by sticking on a used stamp.

Give each child a copy of the photocopiable sheet. Let them write invitations to their friends or toys inviting them to a pretend birthday party. Provide copies of the shopping list to use in the home corner during free play.

Support
Scribe the children's message on their postcard for them, and encourage them to draw their own picture and stamp.

Extension
Suggest that the children choose one form of writing – a list, invitation, letter, postcard or greetings card – and write their own. Offer help if necessary, but let them choose the content and recipient of the writing.

Language and literacy

Learning objective
* To be able to read and write their own names.

Theme links
* All about me
* Letter sounds
* The alphabet

Further ideas
* Encourage the children to talk about their experiences and to listen to others when recounting their experiences by asking each child in turn to tell the story of something that happened during Danny's first day at school.
* Let the children imagine that they are Danny. Instead of behaving in the naughty ways that Danny did, how could they have behaved differently? What do they think he could have done in the playground/at lunchtime/with the blue paint?
* Make up sentences using words with the first sound of the various characters' names. For example: Danny doesn't dribble his drink; Amanda asks Austin for another apple; Baby bounces the blue ball; Grandma gets some green grapes.
* Identify action or doing words in the story. What are the children doing during the course of their day? They are drawing, writing, sitting, standing, running, talking, smiling, shouting, holding, playing and so on.

This belongs to me

Group size: Whole group.

What you need
A large piece of card for each child, with their name written clearly on it (a capital letter, followed by lower case); paper; pencils; tracing paper; paper-clips.

What to do
Refer back to the beginning of the book where Danny writes his name at the bottom of his picture. Why does he do this? Having established that this is necessary to identify it and to stop it getting lost, talk about naming clothes, shoes and other personal belongings, such as books and toys. To be able to do this, children need to learn both how to write and how to read their own names. Give each child the piece of  card with their name on it. Ask them to look carefully at it. Help children to make the link between the first letter written on their card and the sound that is heard at the beginning of their name.

Next, ask them to think whether their name is a long or a short one. Try clapping out the syllables in their names together. For instance, Tom has one syllable and only three letters, whereas Samantha has three syllables and correspondingly more letters. This will help them to be able to 'picture' and therefore identify their own written names. Give each child some paper and a pencil and encourage them to practise writing their own names, copying from the card. If they are having difficulty or if many of the letters are incorrectly formed, suggest that they might like to try tracing over the letters on the card. You may still need to watch over them to make sure that they trace over the letters starting in the correct place and moving in the right direction.

Encourage progression from tracing over letters, to writing over dotted letters, to writing letters independently.

Support
Encourage younger children by linking the initial sound of their names with other familiar objects. For example: Tom likes tea and teddies, Samantha likes sausages and sunshine. Look at ABC books and charts to see the capital letter next to the lower case one.

Extension
Suggest that older children make their own labels for their books and work. Give them some sticky labels and let them write their names onto these, decorating them as they wish.

early years
Story box

Questions and answers

Group size: Whole group.

What you need
Large flashcards of question words: how, when, why, what, which, who, where; a large flashcard of a question mark; a selection of big books, preferably with plenty of questions in them.

What to do
Read the story to the children several times and ask them to identify some of the questions. Many of these ask who did the naughty things in the story, while others ask Danny what he did at school today. We need to ask questions in order to find out about things – who did something, what is happening, how to do something and so on. Why did the dinner lady in the story ask the children questions? Discuss the fact that the dinner lady was trying to find out who had been naughty. Did she succeed? Why not? Is it important to tell the truth? What other questions might the children be asked by the adults in their group? How should they reply?

Look together at the flashcards of the question words. Read them together. Next, look at the question mark flashcard, pointing out its shape. Encourage the children to find other examples of these in the big books. Now take it in turns to ask and answer questions, using different question words. Hold up one of the flashcards, read together what it says and then invite one of the children to ask another child a question using that word. For example, the first child asks: 'What did you have for lunch?'. The second child has to answer using a full sentence, for example, 'I had fish fingers for lunch'.

Support
Practise asking and answering questions without the use of flashcards. Reverse roles and let the children be the adults asking their 'children' questions. If necessary, prompt with topics such as getting up in the morning or having meals. For example: 'Where are your shoes?', 'What would you like for tea?'.

Extension
Introduce the concept of open-ended questions that need more than a yes/no answer. So, instead of asking 'Are you tired?', ask, 'Why are you tired?'. Invite the children to think of open-ended questions to ask each other.

Learning objectives
* To understand why and how we ask questions; to practise asking and answering questions; to recognize the question mark.

Theme links
* All about me

Home links
* Ask parents to encourage their child to look at books. Suggest that they provide an interesting variety of books and teach their child how to handle them properly as well as ensuring that their children see them actively reading and being excited by books.
* Encourage parents to talk to their child and let him or her reply for him or herself. Make sure that they are asking questions or explaining things at a level that the children can understand.
* When reading with their child, ask parents to stop when they are a little way into the story and encourage their child to continue telling the story just by looking at the pictures.

Hair colour

Group size: Whole group.

What you need
Squared paper; pens; coloured pencils; a blackboard or whiteboard; chalks or marker pen; board ruler.

What to do
Begin by looking together at the pictures in *Danny's Picture*. Notice that a number of the children in Danny's group have different hair colour. Danny has blonde hair but his friends have light brown, dark brown, ginger or black hair. The dinner lady has grey hair. Now look at the children and adults in your group. Identify different hair colours within it.

Using the board, show the children how to make a block graph. Draw a separate column for each hair colour seen, identifying each column with a patch of the appropriate colour. Divide each column into squares. Now, go methodically around the room. Note each child's hair colour in turn and colour in one square of the appropriate column. When the graph is completed, it should be clear which hair colour is the most common. Show the children how to interpret the graph by counting the number of filled-in squares. Which hair colour is most/least common? Now, encourage the children to do a tally and to produce their own block graph on the squared paper. Is the result the same as the one on the board? If it isn't, encourage and help them to do some checking!

Support
Let the children record the results of the tally using interlocking bricks in relevant colours. Which is the tallest/shortest tower? So which is the most/least common hair colour?

Extension
Make the graph more complicated by adding a few more variables such as long/short hair as well as looking at the colour. The children will end up with double the number of columns as they record numbers of long and short hair in each colour.

How much will it hold?

Mathematical development

Group size: Four children.

What you need
An old pair of children's wellington boots; plenty of plastic containers, large and small, in various shapes; a water tray full of water; plastic aprons; floor covering.

What to do
This is a messy activity, so start by protecting both the children and the floor! The children are going to use the various items that you have collected to experiment with volume. Begin by looking at the wellington boots. What did Danny do with the boots in the story? Remind the children that he poured paint into Austin's boot. How much paint did he need to fill the boot? Start by suggesting free play in the water tray, allowing the children to experiment with the boots and the various other containers. Encourage them to guess how much water each container will hold. Which do they think will hold the most/least and so on?

Ask the children to imagine that they are Danny. Try filling the wellington boot with water. How much will they need? Which container will provide them with the correct amount of water? Invite them to guess before actually trying. Remind them to think about the shape of the boot – they will need quite a bit of water to fill the toe part before it rises up the leg part. Will any of the containers hold more water than is needed to fill the boot? Encourage the children to think carefully about size and shape. Short, wide containers can hold as much as tall, thin ones even though the tall ones look bigger. How many small containers does it take to fill one of the large ones? How many smaller containers will one large container fill?

At the end of the session, the children should have a better understanding of volume and be more confident in estimating quantities.

Support
Give the children a jug of water and several plastic glasses. How many glasses can they pour out of one jug? Guess and then try.

Extension
Try filling an adult's boot from a child's one. How many times will the children need to refill the small boot in order to have enough water to fill the large one? Guess and then try.

Learning objectives
* To gain an idea of capacity and how shape relates to capacity; to improve estimating techniques.

Theme links
* Shapes
* Water

early years
Story box

7
DANNY'S PICTURE

Mathematical development

Pointed shapes

Learning objective
✳ To be able to draw and identify various shapes.

Theme links
✳ Colours
✳ Shapes

Further ideas
✳ Danny has dinner in school. If he has four friends sitting by him, how many plates, knives, forks and spoons will they need to have on the table? Practise one to one correspondence.
✳ Danny's friends are all special and all different. Always being aware of sensitivities among the children, find out who is tallest/ smallest and who has the longest/shortest hair in your group.
✳ Ask the children: How many naughty things did Danny do? How many nice things did he do? How many times did his picture change, and in what way? (Eyes, mouth, tongue sticking out, star fallen off.)
✳ Encourage the children to experiment building bricks into a tower. Invite them to count how many bricks they have got as they build, adding one each time and telling you the new total.

Group size: Whole group.

What you need
Various large shapes – stars, rectangles, squares, triangles, ovals and circles cut from card or plastic shapes; paper; pencils; self-adhesive silver or gold stars; plenty of gummed shapes including a variety of different types and sizes of triangles, stars, rectangles and so on.

What to do
Remind the children of the beginning of the story where Danny gets a star for drawing a lovely picture. His star has five points. Give each child a gold or silver star and invite them to draw their own. Does it have five points? Do all stars have five points? Show them one that has six. Now invite them to draw a shape that has four points or vertices. They should draw a square or a rectangle. Discuss the difference between these and tell them the proper name for each shape. What is a three-pointed shape called? Can they draw different triangles or are all triangles the same? Point out that all triangles must have three points, then encourage the children to produce as many different shapes and sizes as they can. Talk about other shapes. Do all shapes have points? Discuss circles and ovals. Can the children draw these? Remind the children of the five- and six-pointed stars. Ask them to join up the points on their drawn stars to make sides. Do they know what shapes they have made? Introduce the names of pentagons and hexagons.

Take the children outside and encourage them to look at the front of the building. What shapes can they identify? Look at cars and wheeled vehicles. Why are wheels round? Let the children experiment with the shapes and discover that pointed shapes will not roll, whereas circles will.

Give the children a sheet of paper and a variety of gummed shapes. Invite them to find and stick three shapes with three sides, four shapes with four sides and so on onto their sheet of paper.

Support
Limit the number of shapes for the children to identify. Ask them to find just one shape with three sides, one with four and so on.

Extension
Can the children draw shapes with seven and eight sides – heptagons and octagons? Try making tessellated shape patterns with squares, triangles, rectangles and hexagons.

early years
Story box

Up and down

Group size: Whole group.

What you need
A copy of the photocopiable sheet on page 21 for each child; a model tree made out of a large cardboard roll and green tissue paper (stand the roll upright and stuff some of the paper inside allowing it to 'spill out' over the top); small pictures of a cat, the caretaker, children, Danny and a few leaves, stuck onto card and with Blu-Tack on the back; shoebox; toy car.

What to do
What was the first naughty thing that Danny did in the story? He chased the cat up the tree. The caretaker had to climb up the tree to get the cat down. He ended up hanging upside down, above the children. The leaves that were up on the tree started falling down. The children were playing under the tree. Danny stood beside them. Reinforce this positional language by letting different children place the various picture cards in the correct places on and by your model tree, as you tell them what happened.

Now look around your room. Encourage the children to describe where different items in the room are situated in relation to one another. Begin by describing your position in relation to the children. You might be in front of/in the middle of/beside them. Ask one of the children to describe where the door is in relation to him/her. It might be behind/next to/opposite him/her. Ask the next child a different question. Encourage relevant vocabulary such as inside, on, underneath and between. If the children need encouraging, ask them specific questions about items in the room such as, 'Where are the puzzles?' or ask them to fill in the blank space, for example: 'The books are _____ the table'.

Copy the photocopiable sheet and give one to each child, together with a blank sheet of paper. Help them to cut out the pictures and then encourage the children to stick them in the correct positions around the table.

Support
Help the children to understand the concept of position by providing an empty shoe box and a toy car. Give each child in turn a chance to place the car correctly as you tell them it is in/on/beside/under/behind/in front of the box.

Extension
Ask the children to draw a large picture of themselves. Invite them to add other items to their picture, thinking carefully where those items are in relation to themselves. Can they verbally describe their picture to you, using positional language? For example: 'This is me, my cat is beside me, the sun is in the sky above me, my hat is on my head.'

Learning objective
✳ To understand positional language.

Theme links
✳ All about me
✳ Animals

Home links
✳ Ask parents to use every opportunity to practise counting at home. They could ask how many buttons are on clothes, how many wheels are on the baby's buggy, how many teddies do the children have and so on.
✳ Encourage parents to introduce the complex topic of time by reinforcing the general sequence of events in their child's normal day. For instance: they wake up, go to school, work, have lunch, go home, play, eat tea, their younger siblings go to bed, they go to bed.

Personal, social and emotional development

Learning objective
✳ To understand what is good and right and what is bad and wrong.

Theme links
✳ All about me
✳ People who help us

Further ideas

✳ Can the children remember starting nursery for the first time? Encourage all the children to discuss their feelings at the time. Were they nervous or shy? What, or who, helped them to feel better? What was it like doing other things for the first time, such as swimming or riding a bicycle without stabilizers? Can they describe the feelings involved?

✳ If you have a playground or an area for outside play, encourage the children to look after it. What do they need to do to keep it looking nice? Talk about putting litter in the bin and watering flowers.

✳ Spend time talking to the children about keeping themselves healthy by having plenty of sleep, eating sensibly and taking plenty of exercise. Can the children name some healthy foods? What exercise do they take?

✳ When you have had a messy activity in the classroom, make sure that all the children help you to clear up afterwards.

Right and wrong

Group size: Whole group.

What you need
A copy of *Danny's Picture*.

What to do
Sit the children in a circle. Begin the session by discussing whether Danny was a good boy or a bad boy. Hopefully, you will get the kind of response that allows you to open up a discussion about sometimes being good and sometimes being bad. We all have moments where we are less than thoughtful, less than honest and do things that we regret afterwards. This is normal and not cause for undue guilt or shame. However, it is also important for children to be able to recognize the kind of behaviour that is right and wrong.

Look back at Danny's deeds and decide together whether they are right or wrong and why. Why were the naughty things he did wrong? Talk about being unkind, unfair, dangerous, cruel and selfish. Discuss the importance of telling the truth and the need to own up when we have done something wrong in order to put it right. What were the good things that Danny did right? Discuss being kind, thoughtful and gentle and making an effort. Doing good deeds makes other people feel better and shows that we value, and are prepared to look after, other people and animals.

Discuss rewards and punishments. Danny was given a star as a reward for working nicely. What do the children notice about the star as the picture changes? Danny gradually lost his star because he began to behave badly and do things that were wrong. When he returned home, he gradually got his star back by doing things that were good and right. However, the best reward for good behaviour is the happy feeling it gives us when people are pleased with us. Ask the children when they have done things that they feel good about. Can they remember doing anything that they know was nasty? When people are cross with us for doing wrong, we do not feel nice inside. It is a good idea to try to set targets for improving our behaviour when we know that we have failed in our efforts to be good and do the right things.

Support
Use familiar children's stories such as 'Goldilocks and the Three Bears', 'The Three Little Pigs' or 'Cinderella' to help the children recognize characters which are good and bad. Encourage them to offer suggestions about what the characters have done that makes them good or bad.

Extension
Invite the children to identify some of their own actions which have been both right and wrong. Do the others in the group agree with each child's analysis?

early years
Story box

Getting dressed

Group size: Six children.

What you need
For each child: a cardigan with buttons, an anorak with a zip, a pair of elasticated trouser bottoms, large enough to go over other clothing; two large dice, one numbered 1, 3 and 5 and the other numbered 2, 4 and 6; a pair of wellington boots.

What to do
When Danny had finished being silly at school and was starting to be good at home, he put on his pyjamas all by himself. Tell the children that they are going to play a game together that involves practising dressing skills. Suggest that they take off their shoes and then sit down in a circle. Tell the children that they are going to take turns to throw the dice. When a particular number is thrown, they will all have to perform certain dressing tasks with the minimum of help from you. Begin with the dice numbered 1, 3 and 5, and continue with the dice numbered 2, 4 and 6 when all the items of clothing have been put on. Repeat the game if you wish.
* Number 1 means that they have to put on, and button up a cardigan.
* Number 2 means that they have to unbutton and take off the cardigan.
* Number 3 means that they have to put on and zip up an anorak.
* Number 4 means that they have to unzip and remove the anorak.
* Number 5 means that they have to put on an elasticated pair of trousers over their existing clothes.
* Number 6 means that they have to take off the elasticated trousers.
    Encourage careful thought about the task in hand. Demonstrate how to turn buttons sideways, so that they slip easily through buttonholes, rather than tugging at them which is liable to make them fall off. Ask the children to find the labels in the clothing and point out that these are almost always at the back of clothes. What happens if any of their clothes are inside out? Show them how to turn clothes the right way out. Offer practical help if it is really needed, but try to encourage independence by restricting any help to useful questioning and verbal instructions. Praise the children as they manage to put on and take off the various items of clothing.

Support
Keep it simple by restricting the task to putting on and removing wellington boots.

Extension
Help the children to master the important skills of doing up buckles and tying shoe laces by suggesting that they try, initially, working on each other's shoes. It is easier to get at a partner's shoes than their own, and it is therefore more likely that they will succeed and want to continue trying to do their own.

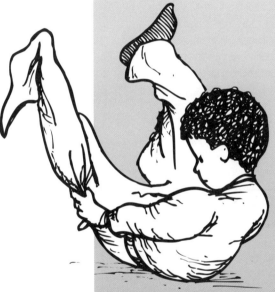

Personal, social and emotional development

Learning objectives
* To gain independence and confidence in doing things for themselves; to be able to manage a variety of clothes fasteners.

Theme links
* All about me
* Clothes

Home links
* Ask parents to help their child to feel comfortable about telling them his or her feelings by always accepting them as valid. They may not agree with them but it is important that they can identify with them. Encourage the children to talk about situations that make them feel happy/sad/frightened and so on.
* Ask parents to reinforce the importance of sharing and co-operating with others during play. They can remind their child that sometimes he or she will lead the play and sometimes another child will.

Cats

Learning objectives
* To learn a little about the features, habits and abilities of cats; to make comparisons with humans.

Theme links
* All about me
* Animals
* Our senses

Home links
* Encourage parents to make a wormery with their child at home by placing a number of worms in a narrow glass container filled with several different layers of sand, soil and leaves. Cover this with black paper and leave for a few days, before looking for trails up against the glass as the worms mix up the layers.
* Ask parents to let children sort through their toys from time to time, and to identify the toys that they no longer play with. Encourage them to talk about growing up and acquiring new skills and interests.

Group size: Whole group.

What you need
Large, clear pictures or photographs of cats, taken at night and during the day; a picture of rock climbers.

What to do
Show the children the pictures of the cats and encourage them to identify the whiskers, tails, claws and fur. In what ways are people different to look at? Talk about the things that cats can do which we can't. Remind the children of the part of the story in which Danny chases the cat up a tree in the playground. Could we run up a tree like that? Why can the cat do it? Describe the role that sharp claws play in enabling cats to grip and climb trees without falling off. If humans want to climb something smooth and steep, they have to wear special spiky shoes and carry spikes, called crampons, so that they can get a grip on the smooth surface. Show them the picture of the rock climbers and identify the equipment that they use to help them climb rocks.

Now talk about the noises that cats make. Can the children make the noise a cat might make as it is chased up a tree? Tell them that cats make this noise when they are frightened. What noise do we make when we are frightened?

Discuss why cats have whiskers. Tell the children that they often hunt at night when it is dark and the whiskers help them to know when they are about to bump into something. If we want to move around at night, we usually have to turn on a light, whereas cats can 'feel' where they are going.

Lastly, encourage the children to look at the shape of the cats' eyes and notice that the pupil changes from being a narrow, vertical slit in bright light, to a diamond shape in the dark. Let the children look at each other's eyes in the light and then in a darkened room and notice the black pupil changing from a tiny circle to a much larger one.

Encourage the children to draw a picture of a cat, labelling the various parts. Draw another picture of a person, labelling all the body parts. Talk about the two pictures and compare them.

Support
Provide pre-drawn outlines of a cat and a person and give plenty of support to label the children's drawings.

Extension
Make further comparisons between a cat and a person. What would we use to climb a tree? How does a cat clean itself? How do we clean ourselves?

early years Story box

Growing up

Group size: Whole group.

What you need
A copy of the photocopiable sheet on page 22 for each child; pictures and photographs of babies, toddlers and young children (ask parents to send in a photograph of their child as a baby).

What to do
Danny has a baby in his family. The baby is too young to go to school, so when Danny goes to school, his baby stays at home with his mother. What other differences are there between Danny and the baby? Talk about things such as walking/being in a pushchair/being carried, talking/babbling, playing independently/needing help to do things, eating/being fed.

   Ask whether any of the children in your group have younger siblings. What can they tell you about them? When and where do the babies sleep? What toys do they have? What do they eat and drink? Babies grow up very slowly. They remain dependent for quite a long time before they gradually become more able to do things for themselves. Before they are ready to go to school, they have to learn how to do many things. Encourage the children to offer suggestions about the things that they had to learn to do, such as walking, talking, feeding themselves and so on.
   Can the children remember anything about when they were babies? Look at the photographs that the children have brought in and talk about how they have changed, then use the photographs to make a display. Conclude your discussion by asking the children what will happen to Danny in the future. Tell them that Danny will grow up into a teenager and then a man. Remind them that everybody grows older, and let them suggest how they will grow and change.
   Ask the children to complete a copy of the photocopiable sheet. Encourage them to draw lines to match the items to the baby, toddler or boy.

Support
Reinforce the concept using teddies or dolls as the baby. Let the children join in some role-play, taking on the different roles of mother, father and child. Perhaps they could have a pretend birthday party to indicate the passing of time and the fact that the baby is growing up, soon to be ready for school.

Extension
Talk about the short passage of time. Can the children tell you what they did yesterday, what they are doing today and what they will do tomorrow? Compare with the longer passing of time, for example the length of time it takes for a baby to grow into a big boy, like Danny.

Learning objective
❋ To learn about the passing of time and to begin to understand the concepts of past, present and future.

Theme links
❋ All about me
❋ Time

Further ideas
❋ Remind the children what happened when Danny poured blue paint into Austin's boot. The blue paint spurted out when Austin put the boot on as there wasn't room for his foot as well as the paint. Illustrate this by showing the children what happens when you put a wooden block into a jug which is full of water.
❋ Talk about the four seasons and the weather today. What season was it in the story? How do we know? What were the children wearing outside? Were there leaves on the trees?
❋ When Danny's picture is on the fridge at home, there is an elephant which has appeared at the top of it. What is it? Why is it there? Talk about magnets and how they stick to other metal things such as the fridge.
❋ Look at the various materials in your room and the materials that the children are wearing. Look for metal legs, plastic seats, wooden tables, wax crayons and so on.

Playground games

Learning objectives
* To learn how to join in and co-operate with others while taking part in group games; to practise controlling their bodies for a variety of movements used in these games.

Theme links
* Ourselves

Further ideas
* Play 'Here We Go Round the Mulberry Bush', putting in suitable actions for recreating the story, such as walking to school, pushing the buggy, drawing a picture, kicking a ball, putting on pyjamas and so on.
* Children often sit in such a way that makes it difficult to produce neat work. Danny has his knees up on the seat of the chair, with his elbows leaning right over the table. Encourage the children to sit with their bottoms on the chair seat, with only their wrists resting lightly on the table. In this position, provided that their chair is at the correct height for the table, they should be able to write and draw with ease and comfort.
* Use modelling clay to make pretend worms. Show the children how to roll the clay under their palm to produce a long, oval shape which gets thinner and thinner the more they roll it. Ask them if they are able to bend their 'worm' into a wriggling shape.

Group size: Whole group.

What you need
A safe, open space.

What to do
In the story of *Danny's Picture*, all the children except Danny – who is chasing the cat up a tree – are playing games together in the playground at break-time. In a safe, open space, encourage your group to do the same. Start by suggesting a game which involves all the children trying to avoid being caught by a child who has been chosen as 'it'. If they fail to get away and are caught, they must stand still with their legs apart until they are freed by someone else crawling through their legs. The game continues until everyone is caught or you decide to change the child playing 'it'. This game relies on co-operation and teaches the children quick reactions. Having to crouch down and crawl through a small space is very good for their co-ordination.

Play 'Follow My Leader'. Let one child be the leader and suggest that he or she leads the others in a series of actions, such as hopping, running and so on as they move around the playground.

Play 'Grandmother's Footsteps' to help the children to develop a good sense of balance. Starting at one end of the playground, encourage the children to move slowly and carefully towards 'Grandmother', played by one of the children. Most of the time, 'Grandmother' will have her back towards the children but she can turn around at any point, in order to try and catch the children in mid-step. The skill is to reach 'Grandmother' first, without being caught moving and therefore having to return to the starting point.

Support
Play 'Here We Go Round the Mulberry Bush', putting in your own words and asking the children to contribute actions. For example: 'This is the way we brush our hair'. Between verses, the children can join hands and move around together in a circle.

Extension
Ask the children to form a circle and give them all a number. Start by throwing the ball to one of the children for them to catch, while shouting out their number. This child should throw the ball to another child while shouting out their number. Continue playing so that all the children have a chance to catch and throw the ball.

early years
Story box

Here we go!

Group size: Whole group.

What you need
A variety of construction kits; large and small junk material; cushions; large paper plates; cardboard rolls; thick, wooden dowelling; cardboard wheels; pipe-cleaners (under adult supervision); glue; sticky tape; string and various fasteners; poster paint; paintbrushes; soft toys and small-world people.

What to do
Remind the children of the part of the story where Danny is trying to be a good boy at home. He has made a car out of a cardboard box with a steering wheel poked through it and is giving his baby brother a ride. Explain to the children that they are going to try to make a car that they will use to take someone for a ride. Ask them to decide whether they would like that person to be a friend, a teddy or a small-world figure. When they have decided on their passenger, encourage them to consider the size their car will need to be. If they are opting for a small model, invite them to design their own, using any construction kits and only offering help if this becomes necessary. Remind them that most cars have four wheels, although some have three.

If a teddy is going to be the passenger, the car will obviously need to be bigger and might be made out of a shoebox, with cardboard rolls or dowelling loosely attached to the bottom with pipe cleaners, so that it can roll along.

For a human passenger, the children will need to think in much bigger terms. They could use large cardboard boxes for the body of the car, cushions for seats, dowelling and paper plates for steering columns and wheels. When the children have finished making their junk model cars, let them paint and decorate them to make them look more realistic.

Support
Encourage very simple designs, using larger construction kits, such as Duplo. If younger children want to make models using junk materials, help them to make holes in the side of their boxes where they can attach cardboard wheels with paper fasteners. This is an easier process than attaching dowelling or cardboard rolls with pipe-cleaners.

Extension
Can the children make a roof for their car to protect the passengers when it rains? If they are using construction kits, they might have to make the car a little wider in order to do this successfully.

Learning objective
✴ To improve manual dexterity while handling junk material and construction kits in order to make model cars.

Theme links
✴ Transport

Home links
✴ Ask parents to let their child help to make their own bed. This is easier if the child has a duvet rather than sheets and blankets!
✴ Encourage parents with children who have younger siblings to let their child help to push the buggy along.

Every shade of blue

* To understand how paint colours are made lighter or darker and to be able to identify different shades of a colour.

Theme links
* Colours
* Our senses

Further ideas
* Explore the sense of touch. What different textures can the children feel in your room? Can they find anything soft, like the cat's fur, rough like the bark of the tree, or sticky like Danny's star?
* Encourage the children to listen carefully. What can they hear inside? Can they hear clocks ticking, bells ringing, plates clattering at lunchtime? Now listen to sounds outside. Can they hear any cats or dogs? What about children talking and shouting at playtime?
* Ask the children to use their eyes to look carefully at the star on Danny's picture at various stages in the story. What happens to it?
* If you serve food in your group encourage the children to smell it before tasting it. Talk about favourite smells and tastes. What do we use to smell with? What do we use to taste?
* Instead of using blue paint, create a blue collage picture, using a wide variety of blue shapes cut from pictures in magazines or old greeting cards.

Group size: Four children.

What you need
Aprons; blue, black and white poster paint; blue watercolour paint; paintbrushes; sponges; items for printing; mixing palettes; white and blue paper.

What to do
Before Danny started being silly with the blue paint, he was painting a nice picture. Explain to the children that they are going to use the blue paint sensibly to create designs and pictures in lots of different shades of blue.

First, ask the children to look around the room and collect as many different blue things as they can. Examine the collection and ask them to grade the items from dark blue to light blue.

Ask the children to suggest how they could create a light blue colour using the three poster-paint colours available. Explain that they will get the lightest colour if they use nearly all white and only a tiny amount of blue and the darkest by adding quite a lot of black to the blue paint. They can create the graded colours in between by using increasing amounts of blue and black.

Encourage the children to experiment mixing the three colours in the palettes. Give each child plenty of white paper and let them paint pictures or design patterns as they wish, encouraging them to use as many shades of blue as they can. Next, invite them to experiment with the watercolour paint. How do they make lighter and darker colours? Explain that the more water they use on their brush, the lighter the result will be. If they use a little water only and really work the brush into the paint block, they will get a much darker and more intense colour. Make a large display of all the children's finished artwork.

Support
Provide several different shades of ready-mixed blue paint. Can the children paint stripes of each one, putting the darkest one first and the lightest last?

Extension
Let the children paint on blue paper instead of white. They will have to think carefully about what shades of blue to use in order that the colours will be visible on the blue background. Again, encourage guesswork and experimentation. Were they right?

early years
Story box

This is me!

Group size: Whole group.

What you need
A copy of the photocopiable sheet on page 23 for each child; large sheets of white paper; pencils; erasers; crayons; felt-tipped pens; poster paints; mixing palettes; water pots; paintbrushes of varying thickness.

What to do
When Danny went to school for the first time, he drew a picture of himself. His picture was a happy one at first, but gradually it turned into a cross one as Danny did more and more naughty things. Explain to the children that they are going to draw pictures of each other. Take care to emphasize that everyone is different and that we all have features that make us special.

Start by grouping the children in pairs, facing each other. Ask them to look very carefully at each other, taking in all the features of the face that they are looking at. Encourage them to pay particular attention to the eyes. What colour are they? What shape are they? Are they just one shape or can the children see several shapes? Point out the black circle (the pupil), the coloured ring (the iris), and the white, pointed oval which surrounds both of these. Look at the eyelids and notice the eyelashes. Now look above the eyes at the eyebrows. Are they dark or light?

Next, concentrate on the mouth area. Look at lip colour and shape. Don't forget the teeth behind the lips. How big is the nose and what shape is it? Now invite them to look at ears and hair. Is the hair curly or straight, long or short? What colour is it? Having allowed quite a long time for careful observation, encourage the children to have a go at drawing or painting each other, including as much detail as possible. Suggest that they use a large sheet of paper so that there is plenty of room for all the features that you have discussed with them. Display the finished portraits on the wall. Can the children guess who is who?

Copy the photocopiable sheet and give one to each child. Tell the children that you would like them to carefully copy the drawing on the left hand side of the sheet in order to make a complete face. Let the children colour in their finished drawings.

Support
Pre-cut the paper into an oval shape and give the children chunky wax crayons for filling in the features of the face. Provide additional paper, scissors and glue for the children to cut out and stick on ears.

Extension
Suggest that the children create self-portraits. Give them a plastic mirror to study themselves in and then invite them to draw or paint themselves, either smiling or looking grumpy.

Learning objective
* To encourage careful observation and accurate reproduction by drawing or painting.

Theme links
* Our senses

Home links
* Being aware of the safety issues, encourage parents to let their children become involved in activities in the kitchen. If parents enjoy baking, they could let their children help to stir the mixture or transfer it to tins. Ask them to point out how the textures change as the different ingredients are blended together.
* Encourage parents to help their child develop an appreciation for music by listening together to a variety and identifying which instruments are playing. Ask them to encourage a sense of rhythm by clapping or moving in time with the beat of the music.

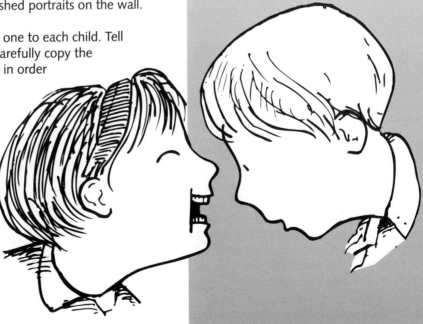

School canteen

Learning objectives
✳ To understand the role of lunchtime assistants, canteen workers and cooks; to be able to lay a table correctly; to appreciate the need for good manners while eating.

Theme links
✳ Food

Further ideas
✳ Make the home corner into a kitchen area. Set out utensils and provide dried ingredients to weigh and measure.
✳ Make a giant car like Danny's with room for passengers in the back. Use cardboard attached to the sides of chairs and add a cardboard steering wheel. Pretend to drive to and from school.

Group size: Whole group to set up the area; nine children at a time to play in it.

What you need
A three-sided screen, with a let-down shelf; four small tables; six chairs; six knives, forks and spoons; six plastic glasses; six plastic plates; large plastic or metal serving dishes; serving spoons; light saucepans; wooden spoons; empty packets of food; three adult aprons; one chef's hat; sticky tape.

Preparation
Begin by making a chef's hat. Cut a band of white card to fit around a child's head. Take several thicknesses of large sheets of white tissue paper and push these inside the band. Tape them to the band in the shape of a chef's hat.

What to do
Talk to the children about canteens in places such as schools and workplaces. Discuss the various roles of chefs, meal servers and lunchtime assistants. Explain to the children that they are going to help you to set up a canteen area in your room.

   Place the screen so that it partitions off a corner of your room, allowing room behind it for the chef to work. Place two of the tables against the middle of the screen, one in front of it and one behind. Place the saucepans and wooden spoons, together with the empty food packets, on the table behind the screen, and the serving dishes, serving spoons and plates on the table in front. By setting up the area in this way, you will be making a kitchen area behind the screen and a canteen area in front.

   Place another two tables side by side in the canteen area, with the chairs around so that you can seat six children. Place the cutlery, glasses and plates on the tables. Allow nine children to play in the area. Choose one to be the chef, wearing the chef's hat and doing the cooking, one to be the server and one to be the lunchtime assistant, patrolling the diners.

   Choose two of the diners to lay the table, putting out a knife, fork, spoon and glass for each of the six places. Now invite the children to line up to get their 'food' from the server, before they sit down and pretend to eat their food nicely, using their knives, forks and spoons in the correct way. (You may need to do some instruction here.) Invite the children to choose some items from your room to use for pretend food to put in the serving dishes.

early years
Story box

Getting to know you!

Group size: Whole group.

What you need
The individual portraits from the activity 'This is me!' on page 17; the A2 poster in this pack; lining paper; mounting card; stapler; guillotine (adult use); glue; individual photographs of the children in your group and one of yourself.

Preparation
Trim the children's portraits and mount these and the photographs carefully onto card.

What to do
Show the children the poster and talk about Danny drawing a picture of himself on his first day at school. Ask the children to share similar experiences of their first day at school. Many of them will have felt nervous or shy. Talk about these feelings together. They usually do not last more than a few days because we begin to feel more comfortable in our new environment as soon as we know more about it and the people within it.

Tell the children that a good way of getting to know other people is by looking at them carefully and trying to remember their faces and names. Once the new faces become familiar, then the children can relax and enjoy themselves, feeling more comfortable in their new surroundings.

Spread the children's portraits and photographs randomly on the table. Sit your group in a circle and show them a photograph of yourself. Talk about your features, such as your hair colour and length, height, eye colour and so on. Now ask the children to look carefully at the group and to identify some of these features within it. To make the situation non-threatening, explain that we all look very different but that we are all very special.

Ask each child in turn to look very carefully at the child next to them and then to go to the table and try to find that child's photograph. Now see if they can find the portrait to match the photograph and put the two together. (You may need to provide help here.) When everyone has had a turn, hold up the pairs so that the children can check whether they are correct.

Use the poster as the central part of the display. Pin the children's photographs and portraits, together with their names, around it. Label the display 'Getting to know our friends'. Let each child put a named, favourite toy on a table in front of the display.

Learning objectives
✳ To be able to match children's photographs to their portraits and to themselves; to help everyone to feel comfortable within a group and to encourage friendship.

Further ideas
✳ Make a display of photographs showing how the children have grown up since they were babies.
✳ Take photographs or ask the children to draw pictures of children and adults showing a variety of expressions, such as happy, sad, angry, surprised, cross, pleased and so on.

early years
Story box

Activity

What shall we write?

Shopping List

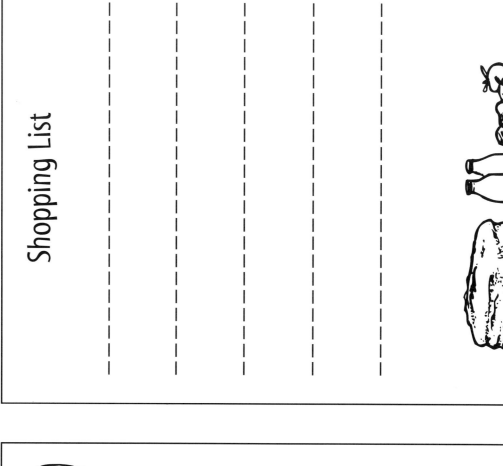

Birthday Invitation

Dear - - - - - - - -

- - - - - - - - - - - -

- - - - - - - - - - - -

- - - - - - - - - - - -

- - - - - - - - - - - -

Love from - - - - - -

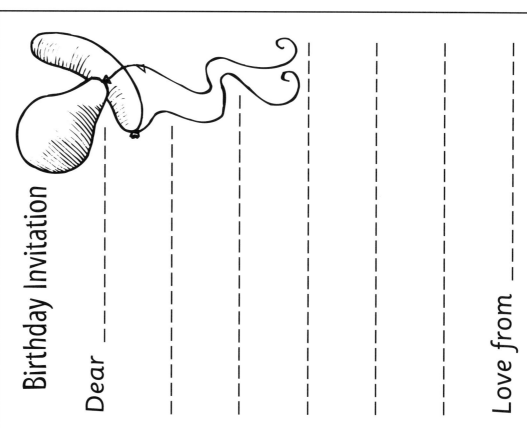

early years Story box

Up and down

Cut out the pictures and stick them in the correct places.

in front of the table

under the table

on the table

behind the table

early years
Story box

Activity

Growing up

Draw lines to join the correct items to the baby, toddler and boy.

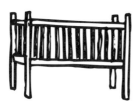  

Photocopiable

DANNY'S PICTURE

early years Story box

This is me!

Fill in the other side of the picture to make a complete face. Colour in your picture.

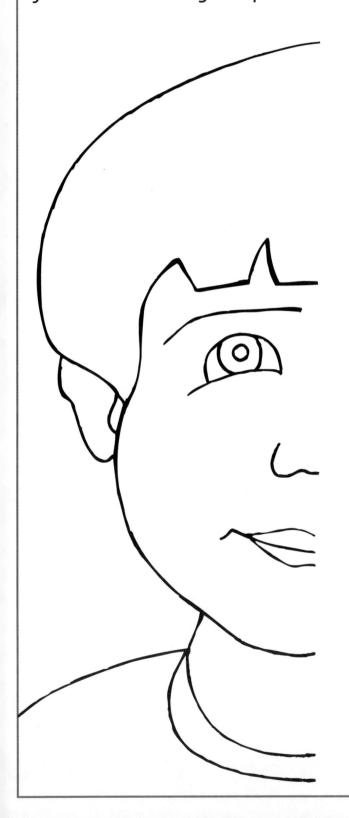

Topic web

LANGUAGE AND LITERACY
* Understand that pictures, as well as print, carry meaning (page 2).
* Look at different forms of writing and write an invitation or shopping list (page 3).
* Make up sentences of words with the same initial letter sound (page 4).
* Practise asking and answering questions (page 4).
* Understand and use action words (page 4).
* Gain confidence in talking and be able to listen to others (page 4).

MATHEMATICAL DEVELOPMENT
* Gather data about hair colour and display it as a block graph (page 6).
* Investigate capacity using different containers (page 7).
* Identify and draw a range of shapes (page 8).
* Use positional language to describe the location of objects in the room (page 9).
* Use comparative language to describe the height of children and the length of hair (page 6).

PERSONAL, SOCIAL AND EMOTIONAL DEVELOPMENT
* Think about how our actions affect other people (page 10).
* Play a game to put on and take off items of clothing (page 11).
* Talk about being nervous and overcoming fears (page 10).
* Discuss ways of keeping healthy (page 10).

KNOWLEDGE AND UNDERSTANDING OF THE WORLD
* Learn about cats and compare them to humans (page 12).
* Think about a baby's needs (page 13).
* Develop an understanding of the passing of time by looking at photographs (page 13).

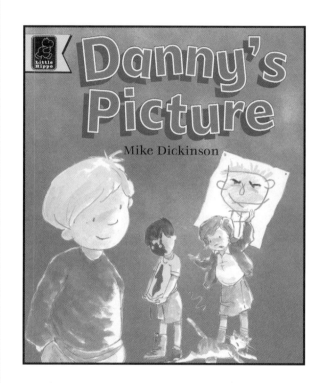

PHYSICAL DEVELOPMENT
* Join in some playground games with the rest of the group (page 14).
* Use a variety of movements to play games (page 14).
* Make a car out of a construction kit or junk material (page 15).
* Make wiggly worms by rolling out lengths of Plasticine (page 14).
* Practise sitting properly at a table (page 14).

CREATIVE DEVELOPMENT
* Mix colours together to create different shades of blue (page 16).
* Make a collage picture by cutting pieces from magazines (page 16).
* Draw a portrait of a friend after studying their face carefully (page 17).
* Use the senses of hearing and touch to investigate different sounds and textures (page 16).

Photocopiable

24

DANNY'S PICTURE

early years
Story box

Danny's Picture

Mike Dickinson

Little
Hippo

One morning Danny woke up early.
It was a special day. It was his very
first day at school.

Mummy and the baby took him there.
"Now be a good boy, won't you, Danny?"
said Mummy as she waved goodbye.

Danny went into the classroom and sat down at his table.

He drew a picture of himself and wrote his name in big letters at the bottom.

Danny was very pleased with his picture.
It looked just like him. He showed the
picture to his teacher.

"Very good," she said. "It deserves a
gold star." The teacher pinned Danny's
picture on the classroom wall.

At break-time Danny went out into the
playground. He scared the school cat and
chased her up a tree.

The school caretaker climbed up
the tree and rescued her.
"Who frightened the cat?" he asked.
"Not me," smiled Danny.

In the classroom on the wall Danny's picture began to change. It looked a little bit different now.

At lunchtime, Danny sat next to Amanda.
He dropped a dried-up worm into her
custard when she wasn't looking.

When Amanda found the worm she
screamed and screamed. The dinner
lady had to clean up the mess.
"Who did that?" she said.
"It wasn't me," grinned Danny.

In the classroom on the wall Danny's picture changed again. It looked very different now.

When it was time to go home, Danny poured blue paint into one of Austin's wellington boots.

Austin put on his boot and the paint splashed everywhere.

Austin's mother was very cross.

"Who did that?" she said.

"Not me," smirked Danny.

In the classroom on the wall Danny's picture changed again. It looked completely different. Was it really Danny?

Mummy and the baby came to take
Danny home.

"What did you do at school today?"
asked Mummy.
Danny showed Mummy his picture.

When they got home, Danny's
Mummy looked at the picture again.
"What a horrid little monster!" said
Mummy and she stuck Danny's
picture on the fridge door.

At teatime somebody saved the cat
from the dog next door.

"Who saved the cat?" said Mummy.

"It was me," said Danny.

In the kitchen, on the fridge door,
Danny's picture began to change.

After tea someone gave the baby a ride
in their car.

"Ah," said Mummy, "Now who did that?"
"I did," said Danny. "I gave the baby a ride."

In the kitchen, on the fridge door, Danny's picture changed again.

At bedtime, someone put their pyjamas on all by themselves.

"Who did that?" asked Mummy.

"It was me," smiled Danny.

In the kitchen, on the fridge door, Danny's picture looked just like Danny once more.

Grandma called in to say goodnight. "What did Danny do at school today?" asked Grandma.

"He drew a horrid little monster. I stuck it on the fridge door," said Mummy.

When Grandma saw the picture she laughed. "That's not a horrid little monster," said Grandma. "It's Danny!"

"Danny's not a monster. He's a good boy, aren't you?" beamed Grandma.

"I will be tomorrow," said Danny.

This Little Hippo
book belongs to

_____

_____

Scholastic Children's Books,
Commonwealth House, 1-19 New Oxford Street
London WC1A 1NU, UK
a division of Scholastic Ltd

London • New York • Toronto • Sydney • Auckland
Mexico City • New Delhi • Hong Kong

First published in the UK in 1998 by Little Hippo,
an imprint of Scholastic Ltd

Copyright © Mike Dickinson 1998

ISBN 0 590 19988 9

Printed in Italy